Highlights

HANDWRITING
Tracing Practice

For full classroom solutions and to learn why handwriting is a key foundational skill for literacy development, visit www.zaner-bloser.com/handwriting2020.

Published by Highlights Learning • 815 Church Street • Honesdale, Pennsylvania 18431
ISBN: 978-1-68437-661-2
Printed in Dongguan City, Guangdong, China
Mfg. 03/2019

First edition
10 9 8 7 6 5 4 3 2 1

For assistance in the preparation of this book, the editors would like to thank:
The handwriting experts at Zaner-Bloser, leaders in language arts education for more than 125 years
Vanessa Maldonado, MSEd; MS Literacy Ed. K–12; Reading/LA Consultant Cert.; K–5 Literacy Instructional Coach

Welcome!

This book belongs to:

Draw a picture of yourself here.

Trace the letters in your name.

Can you write your name? Write it below.

Go Left

Trace your left hand on this mitten.

Which hand do you use to hold your pencil?

Trace the line from each hat to its matching mittens or gloves.

Circle the hat that has a bow. Draw a square around the mittens that have stripes.

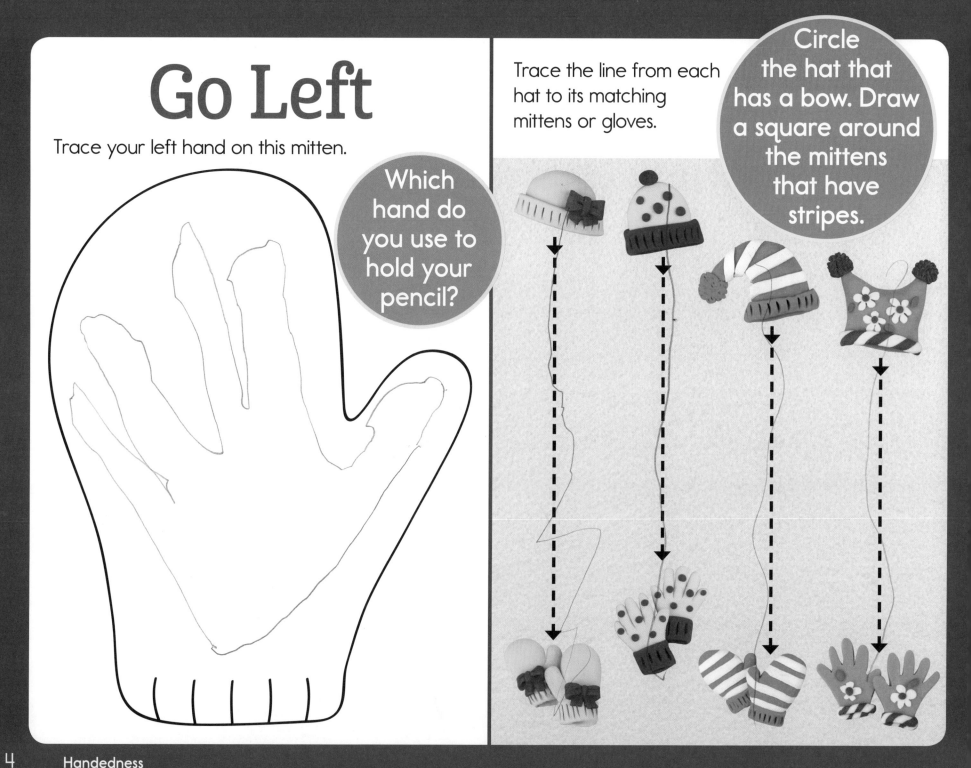

Right Here

Trace your right hand on this mitten.

Find and circle the **5** mittens hidden in the picture. Color in a mitten for each one you find.

Writing Positions

Left-Handed Writers If you use your left hand to write, follow the rules on this page.

Sit up tall. Keep your feet flat on the floor.

Digital Tutor:
Pencil Position

Digital Tutor:
Sitting Position

Hold the pencil like this.

Do not squeeze the pencil when you write.

Digital Tutor

Scan the Digital Tutor codes with a mobile device to watch videos. You will learn how to sit and hold your pencil while writing.

Right-Handed Writers

If you use your right hand to write, follow the rules on this page.

Sit up tall. Keep your feet flat on the floor.

Digital Tutor:
Sitting Position

Digital Tutor:
Pencil Position

Hold the pencil like this.

Do not squeeze the pencil when you write.

Models and Guidelines

Arrows show how to write letters.

Start at the ●.

Pull Down Lines

Trace and write the pull down lines. Start at the ●.

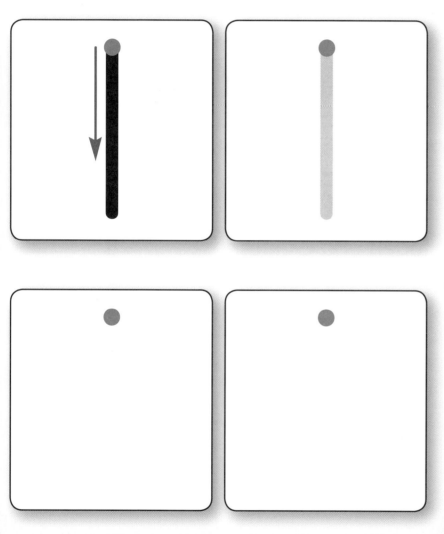

Trace the lines from the balloons to the kids. Whose balloon is orange?

Slide Lines

Trace and write the slide lines. Start at the ●.

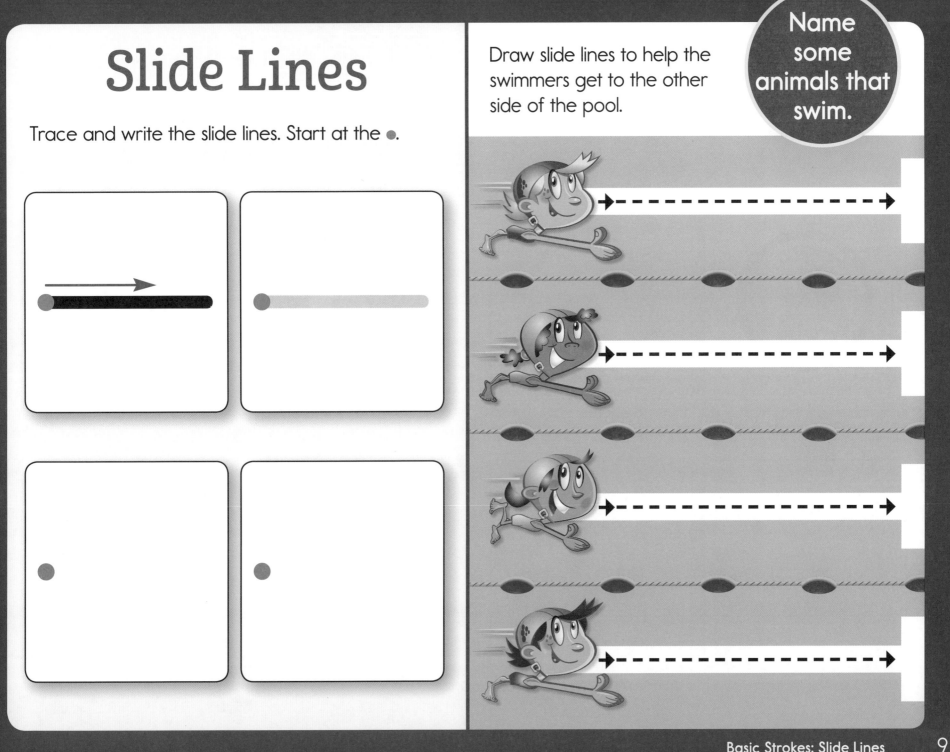

Draw slide lines to help the swimmers get to the other side of the pool.

Name some animals that swim.

Backward Circle Lines

Trace and write the backward circle lines.
Start at the ●.

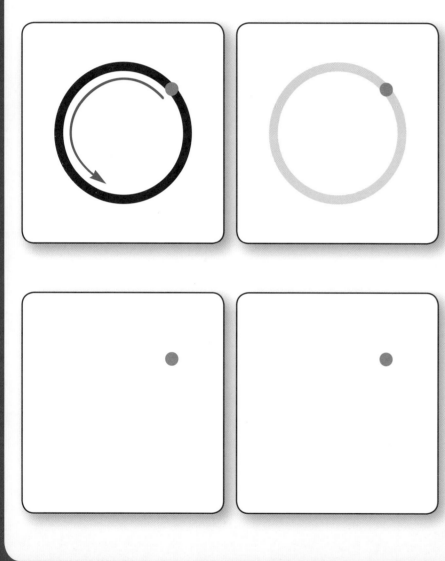

What silly things do you see?

Trace the backward circle lines in this picture.

Forward Circle Lines

Trace and write the forward circle lines.
Start at the ●.

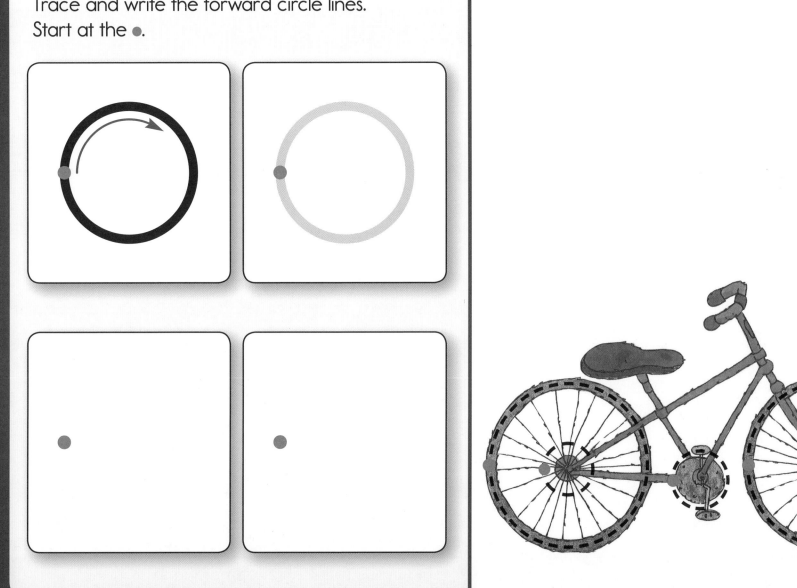

Slant Lines: Down

Trace and write the slant down lines. Start at the ●.

Trace the slant down lines to help each spaceship get to its planet.

Which planet would you like to visit? Why?

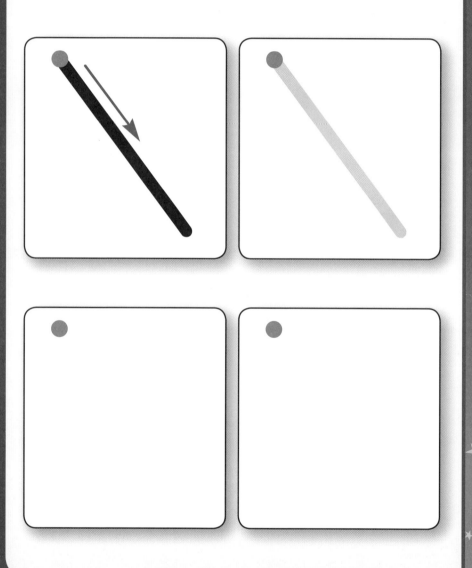

Slant Lines: Up

Trace and write the slant up lines. Start at the ●.

Trace the slant up lines from each bowler to the ball.

How many bowling balls do you see? Circle the bowling ball that is a different color.

Write A

Trace and write the letter A. Start at the ●.

Draw a line from each animal to its toy.

Which toy would you play with?

Write B

Trace and write the letter B. Start at the •.

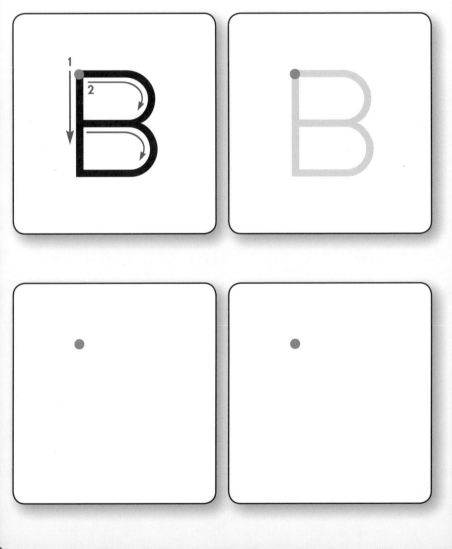

BLUE	BROWN	BLACK	YELLOW
■	▲	★	●

Write C

Trace and write the letter C. Start at the ●.

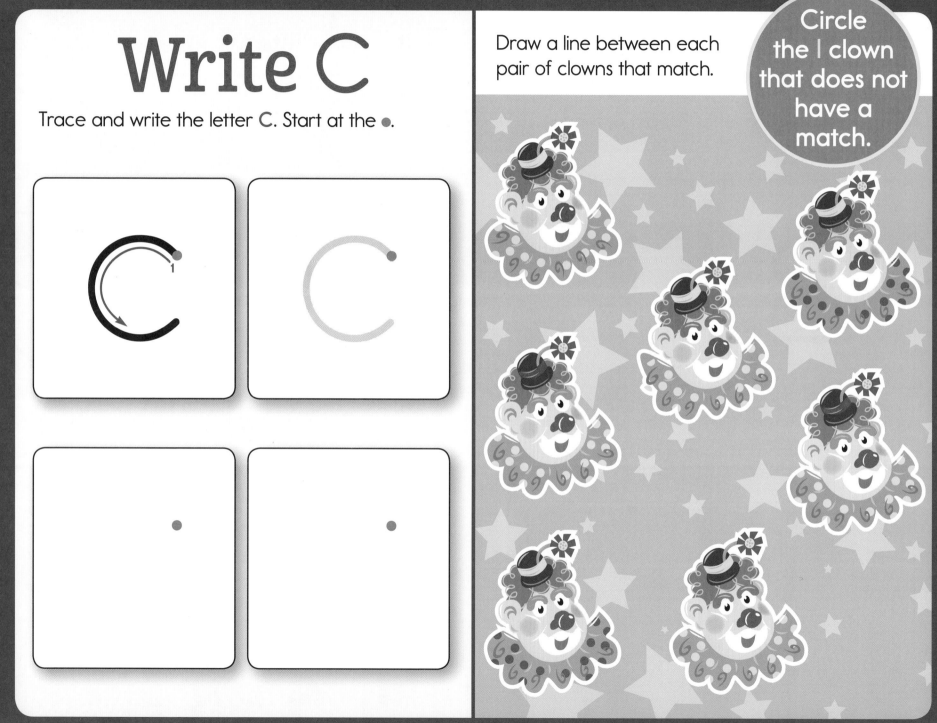

Draw a line between each pair of clowns that match.

Circle the 1 clown that does not have a match.

Write D

Trace and write the letter D. Start at the ●.

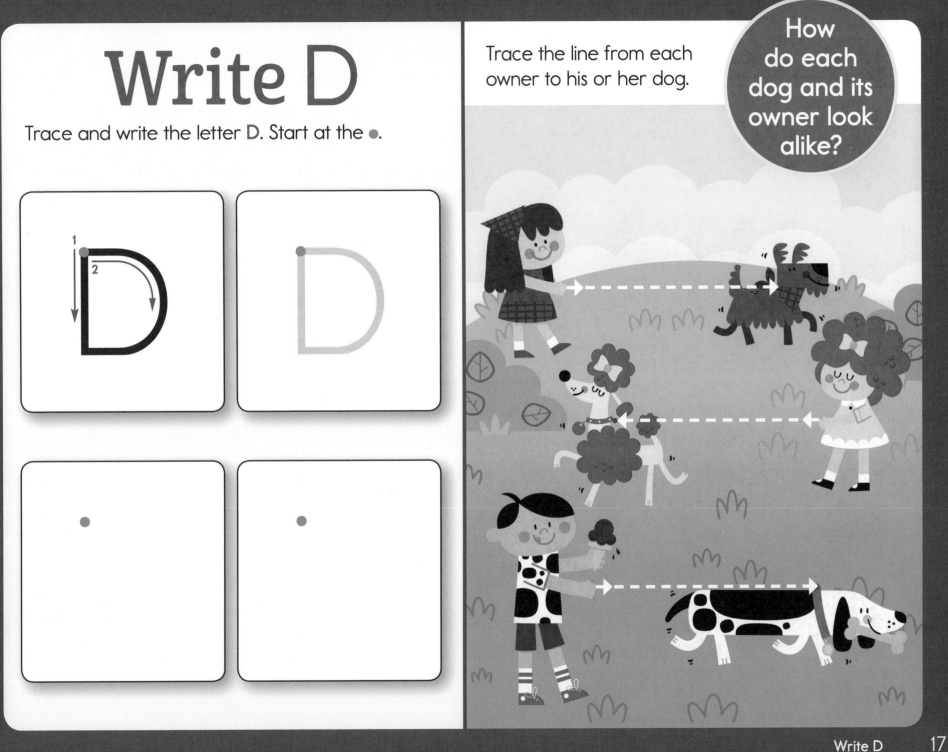

Trace the line from each owner to his or her dog.

How do each dog and its owner look alike?

Write E

Trace and write the letter E. Start at the ●.

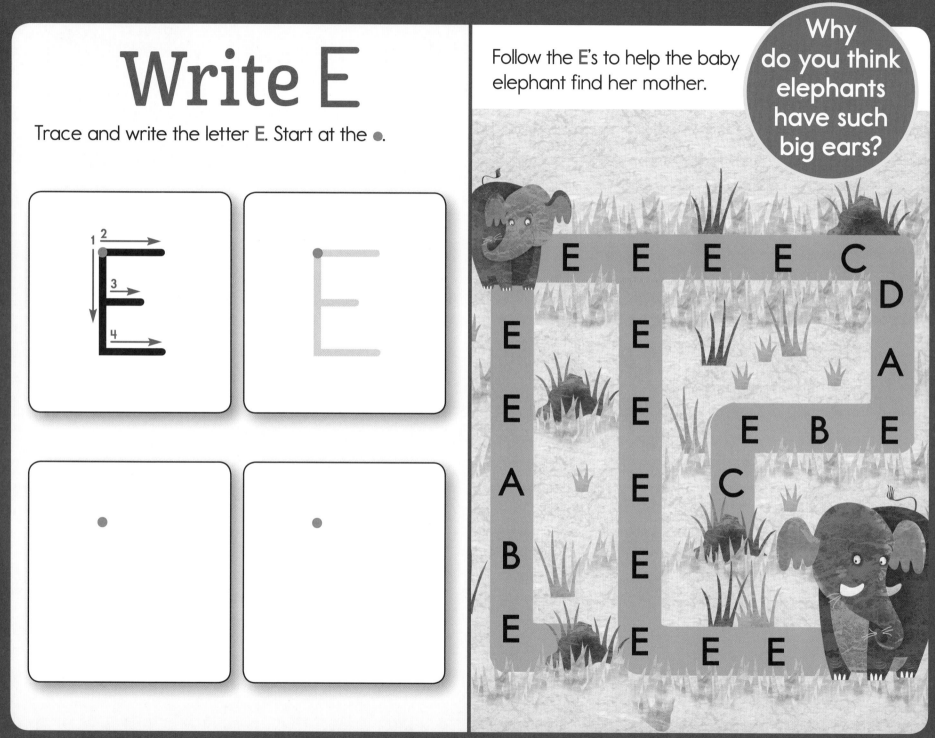

Follow the E's to help the baby elephant find her mother.

Why do you think elephants have such big ears?

Write F

Trace and write the letter F. Start at the ●.

Draw a line from each frog to its leaf.

Write G

Trace and write the letter G. Start at the ●.

Draw a line between each pair of matching giraffes.

Why do you think giraffes have long necks?

Write H

Trace and write the letter H. Start at the ●.

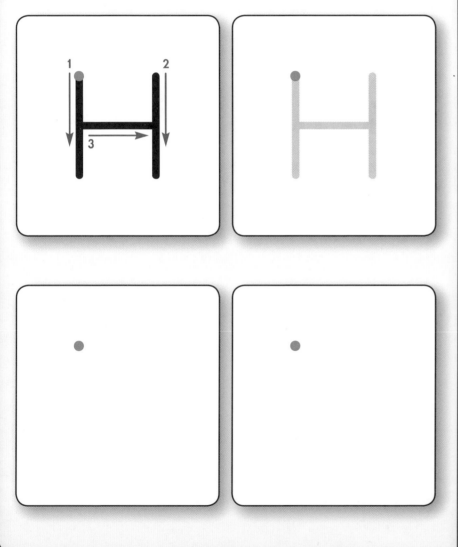

What would you serve at your party?

Write I

Trace and write the letter I. Start at the •.

Draw a line from each kid to his or her ice-cream soda.

What's your favorite ice-cream topping?

Write J

Trace and write the letter J. Start at the ●.

J

J

Trace the lines to finish the jump ropes.

Name some animals that jump.

Write K

Trace and write the letter K. Start at the ●.

Draw a string from each kid to his or her kite.

What other things can fly high?

Write L

Trace and write the letter L. Start at the ●.

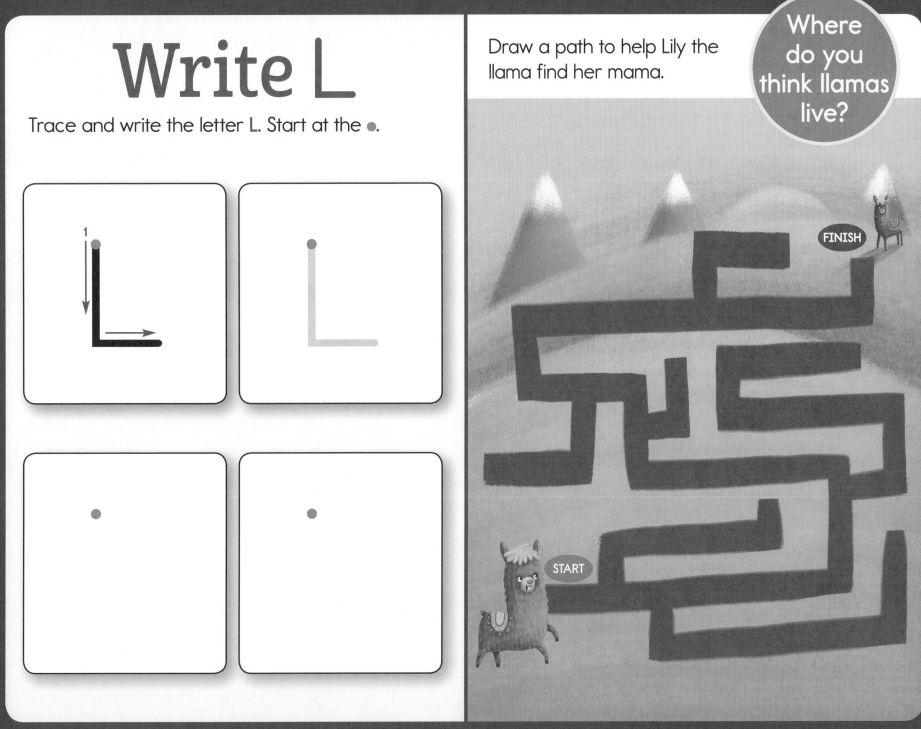

Draw a path to help Lily the llama find her mama.

Where do you think llamas live?

FINISH

START

Write M

Trace and write the letter M. Start at the ●.

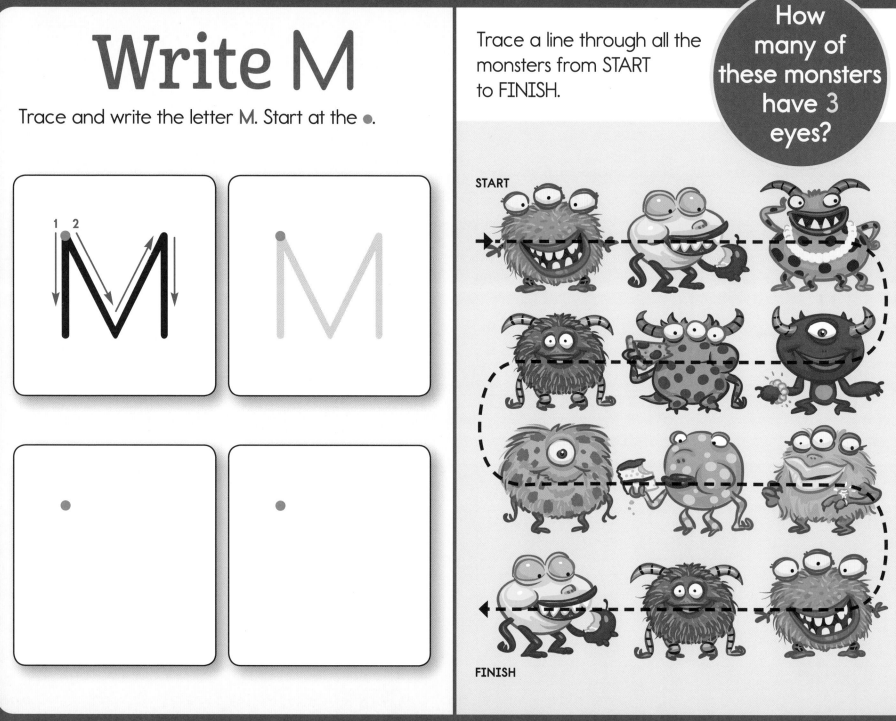

Trace a line through all the monsters from START to FINISH.

How many of these monsters have 3 eyes?

START

FINISH

Write N

Trace and write the letter N. Start at the ●.

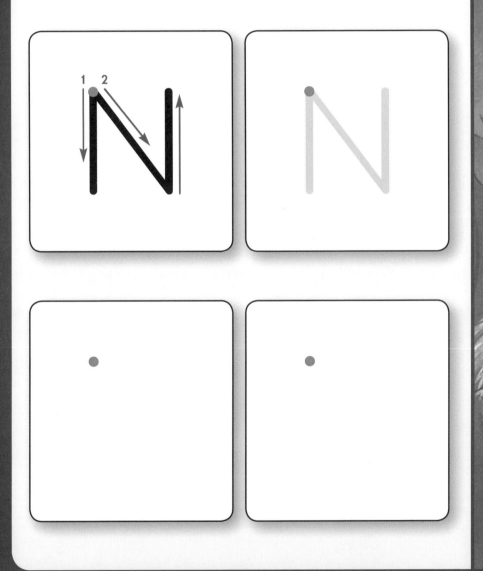

Trace each N you see near this nice nest.

What do animals use to make their nests?

Write O

Trace and write the letter O. Start at the ●.

Draw a line between each pair of matching octopuses.

How many legs does an octopus have?

Write P

Trace and write the letter P. Start at the •.

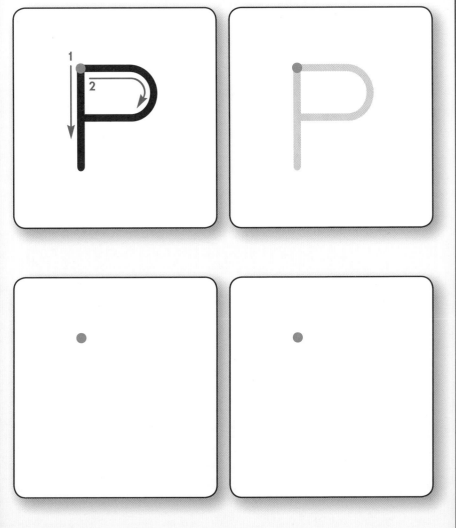

Trace the lines to finish the playground in the park. Then draw a sun and more clouds in the sky.

Which person has a puppy?

Write Q

Trace and write the letter Q. Start at the ●.

Count the Q's in Quinta's room. Cross off as you count.

What patterns do you see in Quinta's room?

Write R

Trace and write the letter R. Start at the ●.

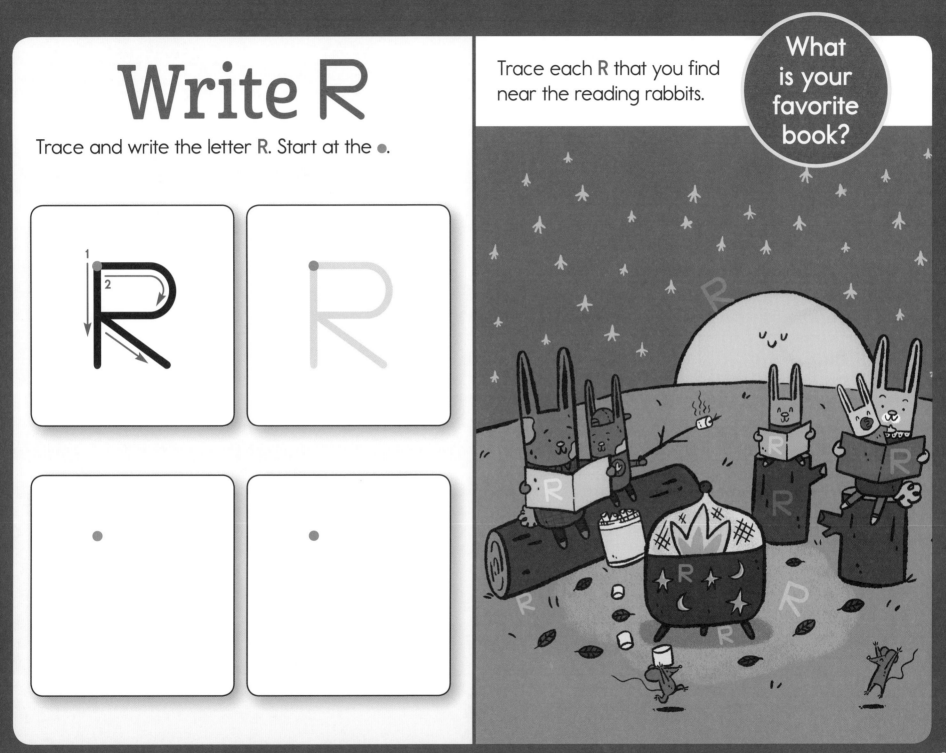

Trace each **R** that you find near the reading rabbits.

What is your favorite book?

Write S

Trace and write the letter S. Start at the ●.

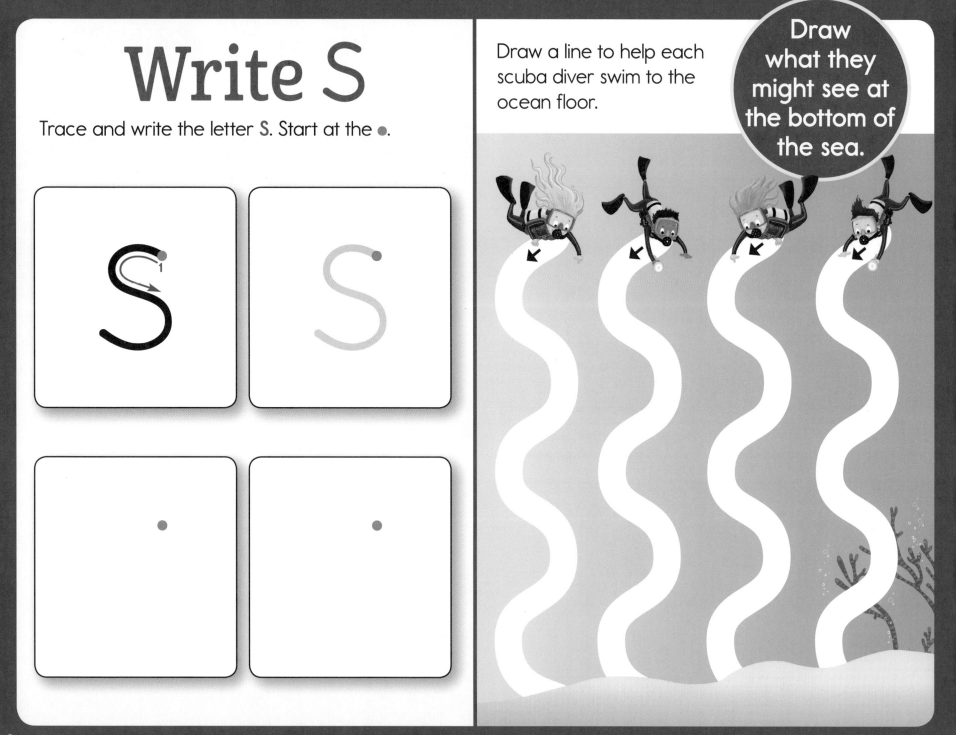

Draw a line to help each scuba diver swim to the ocean floor.

Draw what they might see at the bottom of the sea.

Write T

Trace and write the letter T. Start at the •.

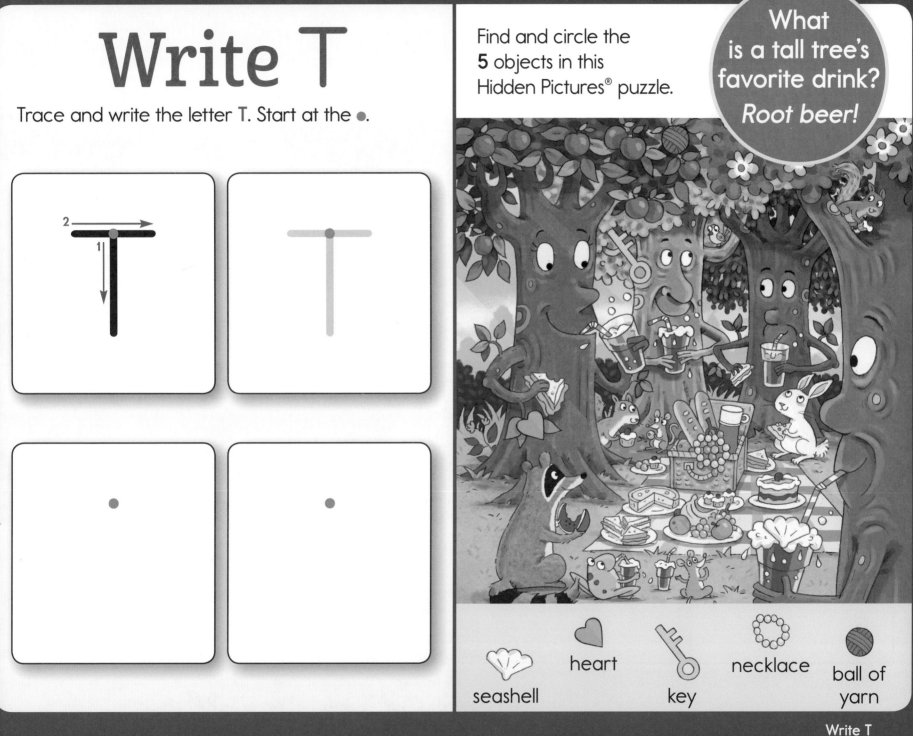

What is a tall tree's favorite drink? *Root beer!*

seashell
heart
key
necklace
ball of yarn

Write U

Trace and write the letter U. Start at the ●.

Trace the lines to finish the umbrellas and rainbow.

Which umbrellas have polka dots?

Write V

Trace and write the letter V. Start at the ●.

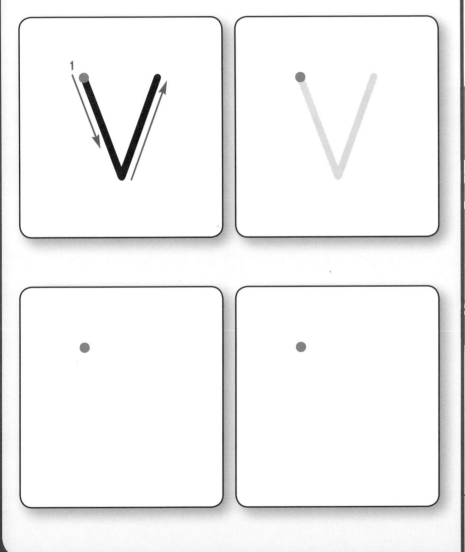

Find **10** hearts at this Valentine's Day party. Trace and color the hearts below as you find them.

Write W

Trace and write the letter W. Start at the ●.

Where does each ball go? Trace the lines to find out.

Why do different sports use different balls?

Write X

Trace and write the letter X. Start at the •.

Draw an **X** to cross out the dessert in each row that isn't the same as the others.

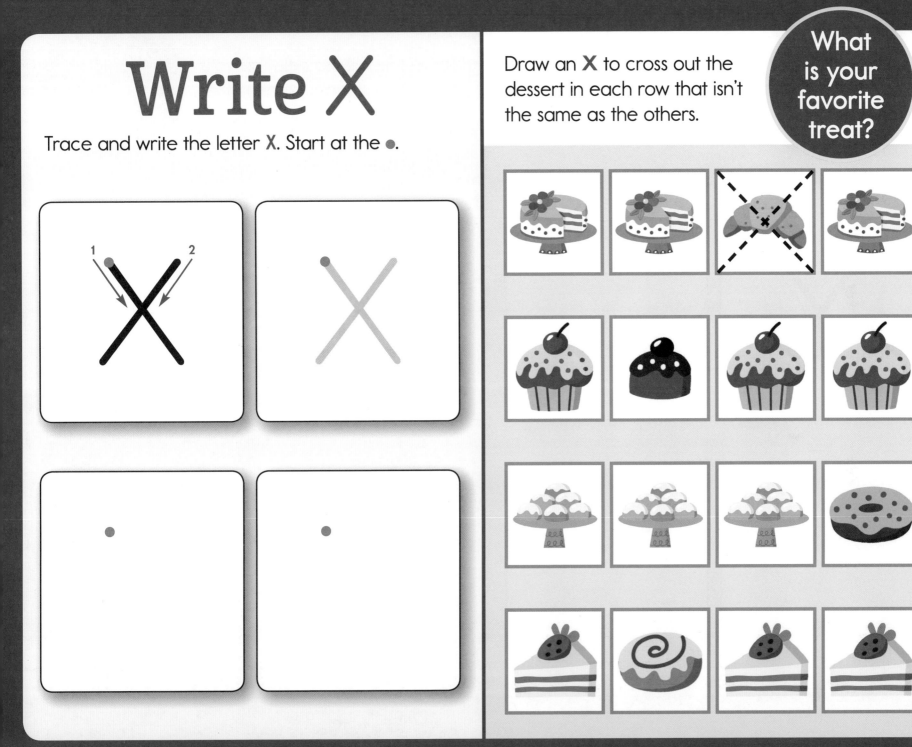

Write Y

Trace and write the letter Y. Start at the ●.

Trace the lines to help the yaks bring their kayaks to the river.

Which kayak is yellow?

Write Z

Trace and write the letter Z. Start at the ●.

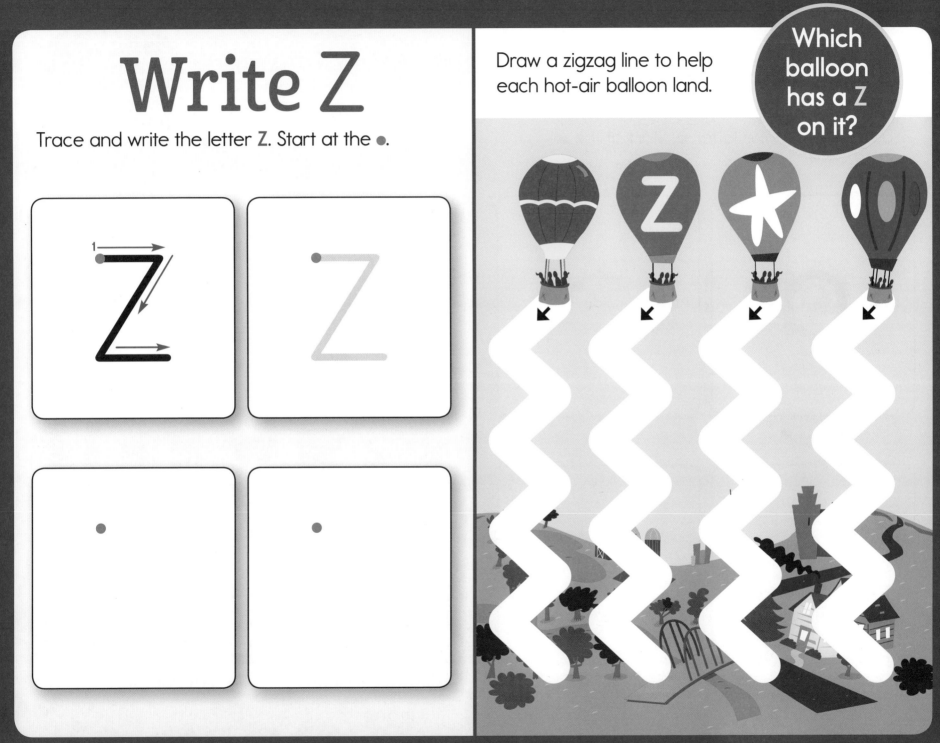

Draw a zigzag line to help each hot-air balloon land.

Which balloon has a Z on it?

Write a

Trace and write the letter a. Start at the ●.

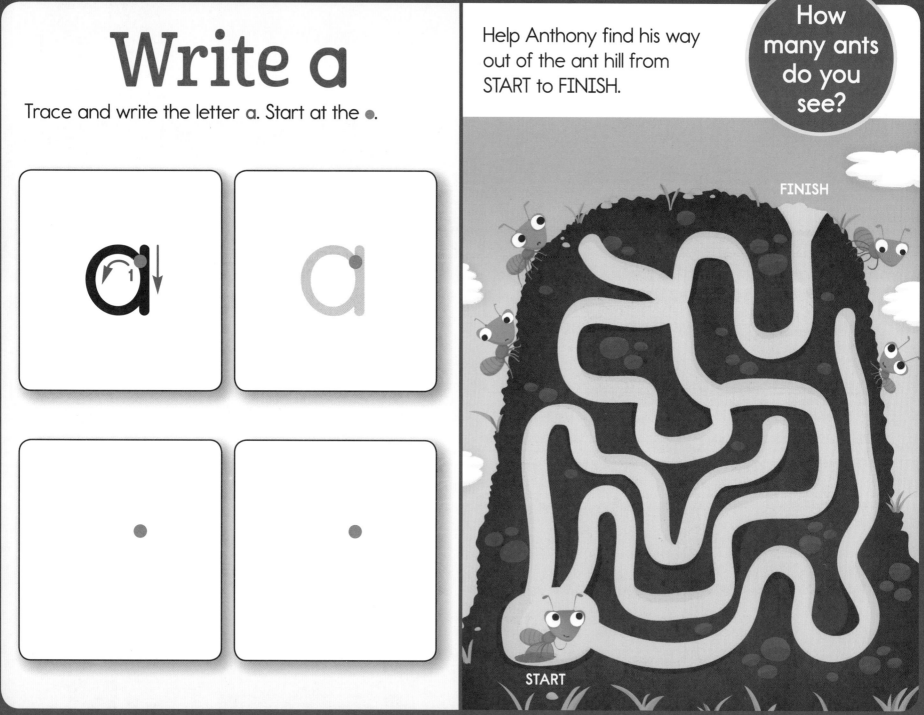

Help Anthony find his way out of the ant hill from START to FINISH.

How many ants do you see?

FINISH

START

Write b

Trace and write the letter b. Start at the •.

Find and circle the **6** objects that begin with the letter **b** in this Hidden Pictures® puzzle.

bagel

ball of yarn

bowling ball

basketball

button

bull's-eye

Write c

Trace and write the letter c. Start at the ●.

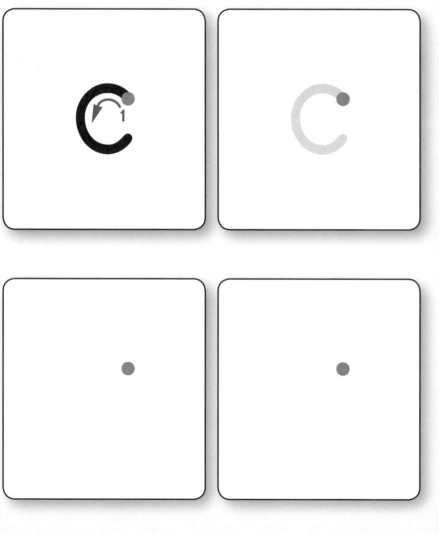

Write d

Trace and write the letter d. Start at the ●.

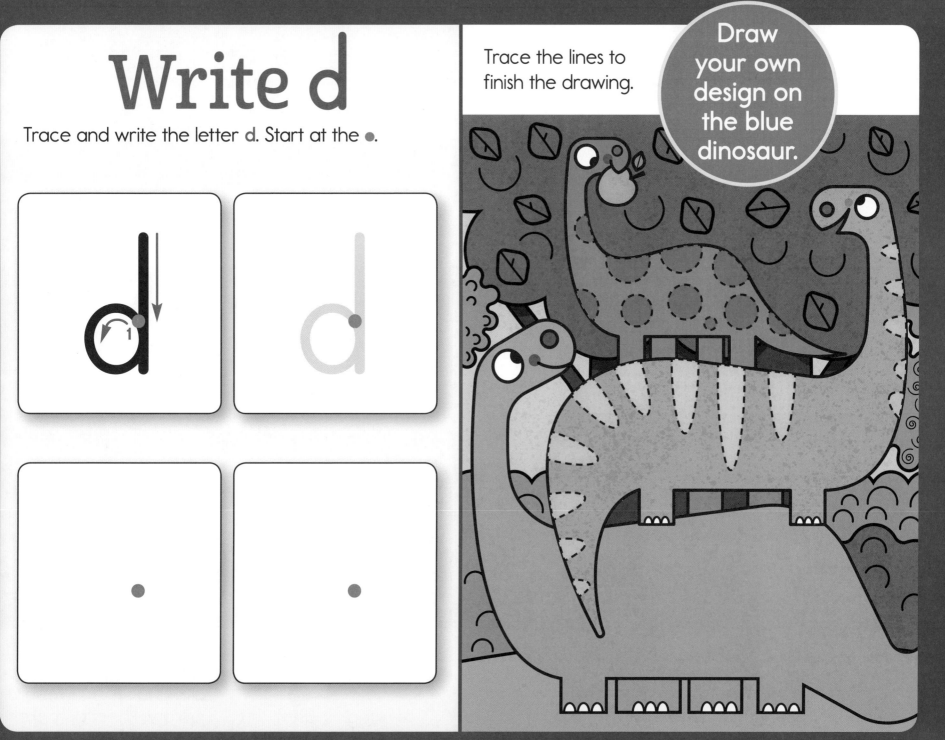

Trace the lines to finish the drawing.

Draw your own design on the blue dinosaur.

Write e

Trace and write the letter e. Start at the ●.

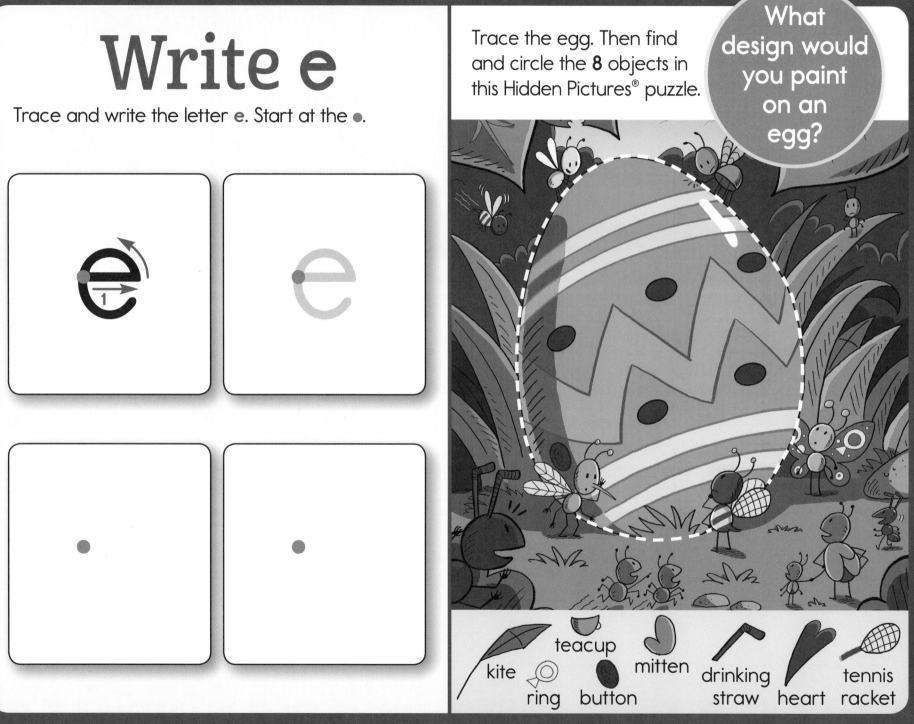

Trace the egg. Then find and circle the **8** objects in this Hidden Pictures® puzzle.

What design would you paint on an egg?

kite
teacup
mitten
ring
button
drinking straw
heart
tennis racket

Write f

Trace and write the letter f. Start at the •.

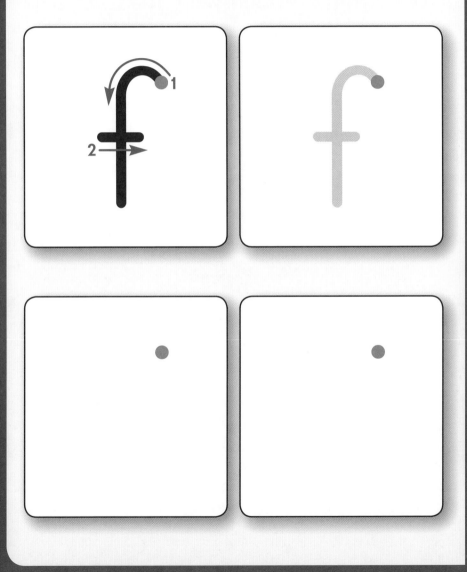

Find and circle the **5** objects in this Hidden Pictures® puzzle.

What do you find funny about these fish?

comb   doughnut   bread   srewdriver   saw

Write g

Trace and write the letter g.
Start at the ●.

Trace the yarn to see which gift each animal is knitting.

Write h

Trace and write the letter h. Start at the ●.

1

What's hiding in this hole? Trace the **h**, and then use the shape to draw something hiding there.

Write i

Trace and write the letter i. Start at the •.

2•
1↓

Find and color the **6** objects in this Hidden Pictures® puzzle.

Name 4 flavors of ice cream.

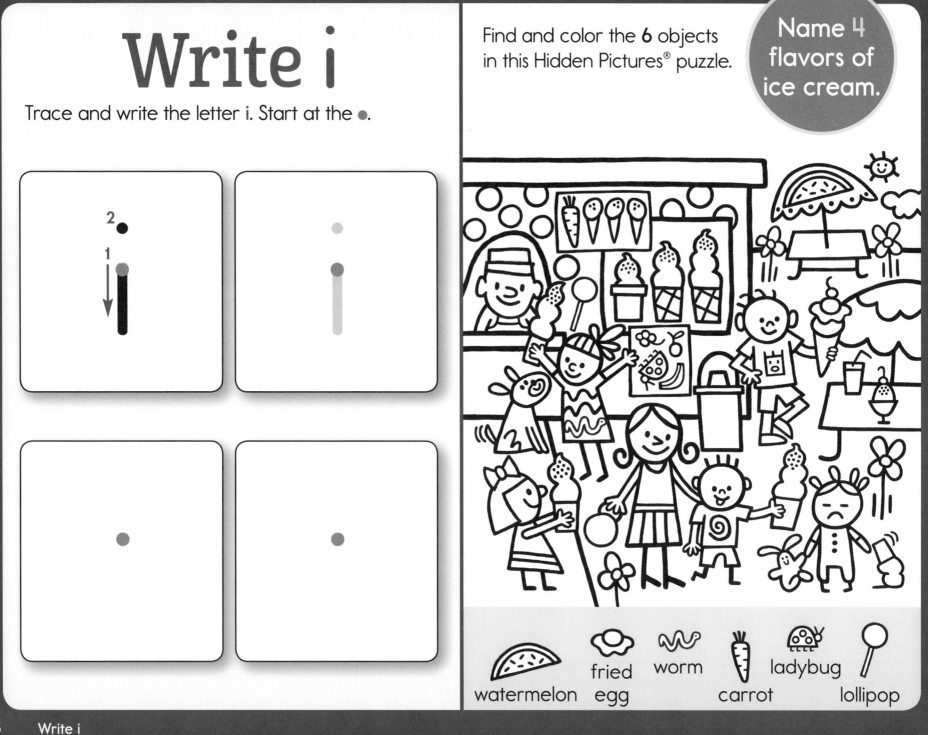

watermelon   fried egg   worm   carrot   ladybug   lollipop

Write j

Trace and write the letter j.
Start at the ●.

2
1
j

Help Jamie and Jimmy find the j's in the jungle. Trace each one you find.

What animals live in the jungle?

Write k

Trace and write the letter k. Start at the ●.

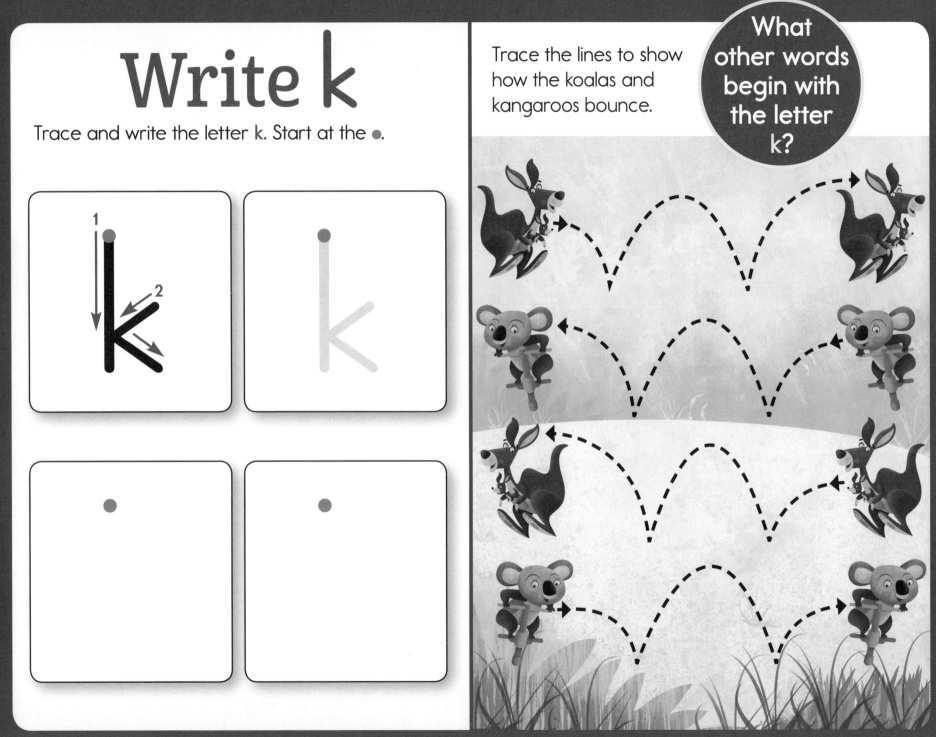

Trace the lines to show how the koalas and kangaroos bounce.

What other words begin with the letter k?

Write l

Trace and write the letter l. Start at the ●.

1
↓

Which ladder is the shortest? Which ladder is the tallest?

Draw a line to help each construction worker reach the ground.

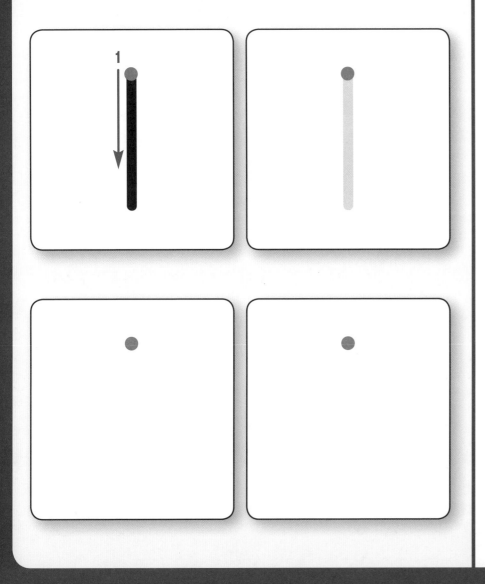

Write m

Trace and write the letter m. Start at the ●.

Draw a line between each pair of monkeys.

Circle the 2 monkeys that are wearing the same clothes.

Write n

Trace and write the letter n. Start at the ●.

Trace the lines to finish the drawing. Color the squirrel and nuts.

What other animals eat nuts?

Write o

Trace and write the letter o. Start at the ●.

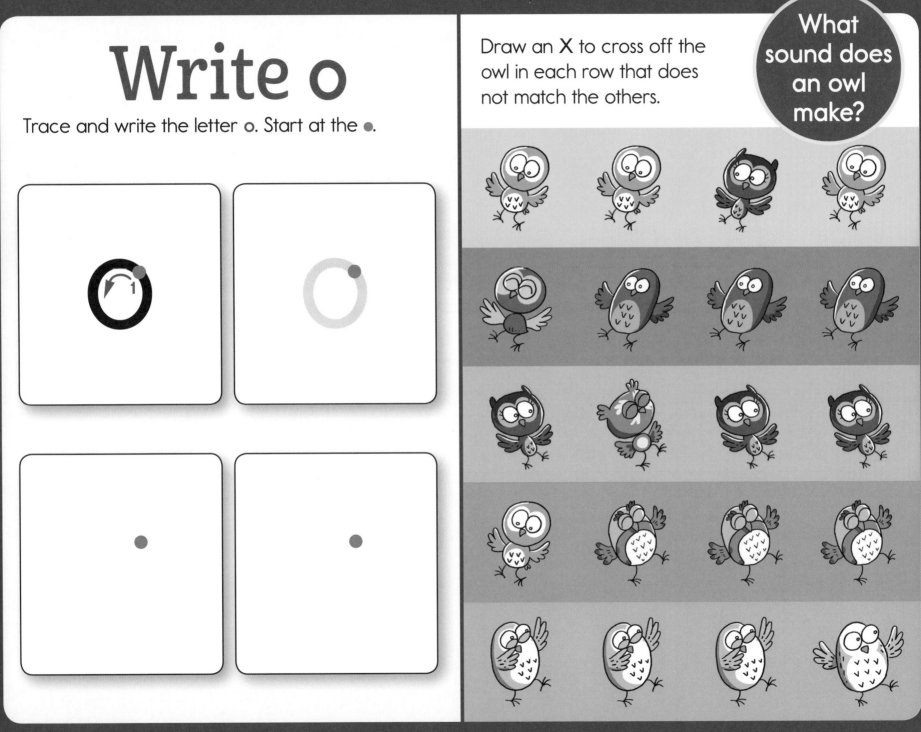

Draw an **X** to cross off the owl in each row that does not match the others.

What sound does an owl make?

Write p

Trace and write the letter p.
Start at the ●.

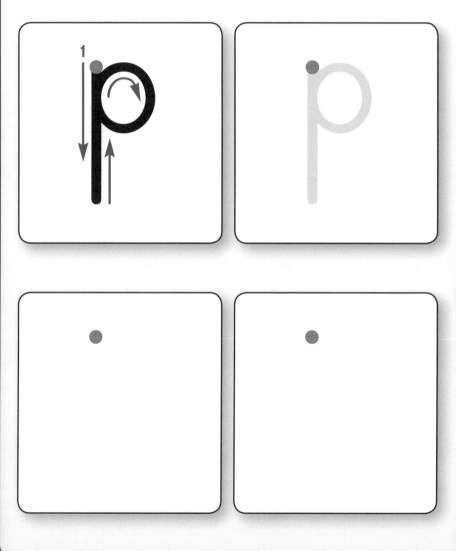

Find and circle the **7** objects that begin with the letter p in this Hidden Pictures® puzzle.

pumpkin   pen   paper airplane   pie

penny   pizza cutter   pancake

Write q

Trace and write the letter q.
Start at the ●.

Follow the q's to help the queen return to her throne.

How many crowns do you see?

Write r

Trace and write the letter r. Start at the ●.

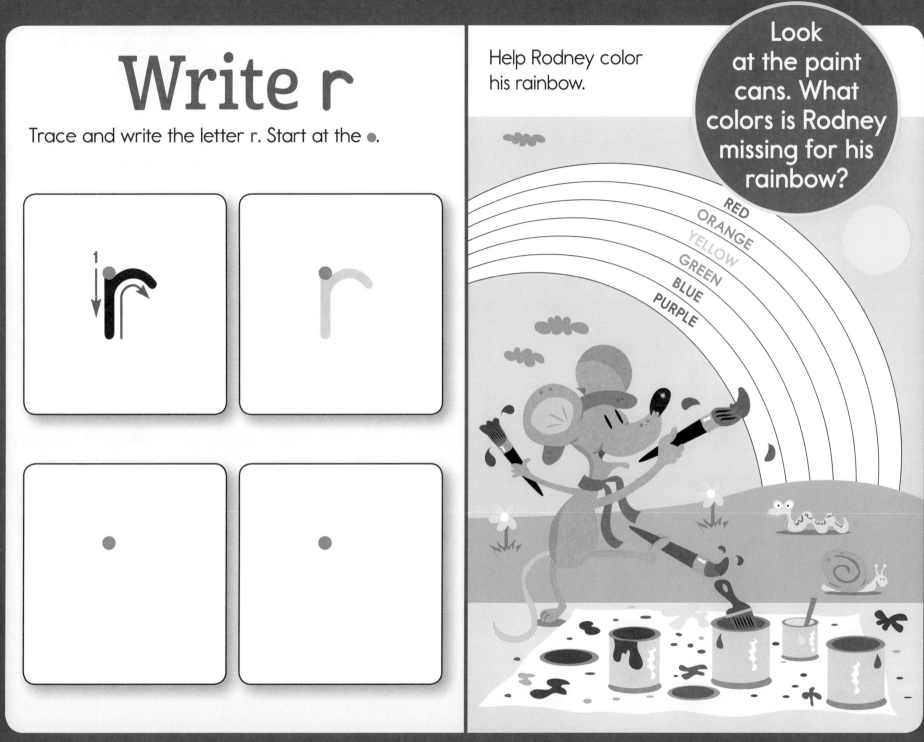

Help Rodney color his rainbow.

Look at the paint cans. What colors is Rodney missing for his rainbow?

RED
ORANGE
YELLOW
GREEN
BLUE
PURPLE

Write s

Trace and write the letter s. Start at the ●.

S¹

s

Draw a line between the 2 snowmen that are the same.

Trace the s and then use the shape to draw your own snowman.

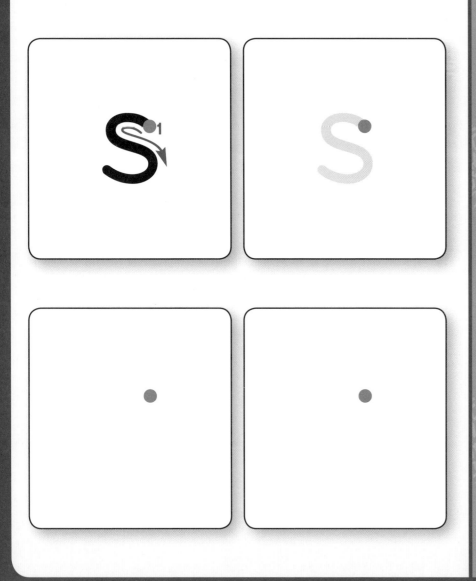

S

Write t

Trace and write the letter t. Start at the ●.

Draw a path to help the tractor reach the barn.

What things might grow on a farm?

START

FINISH

Write u

Trace and write the letter u. Start at the ●.

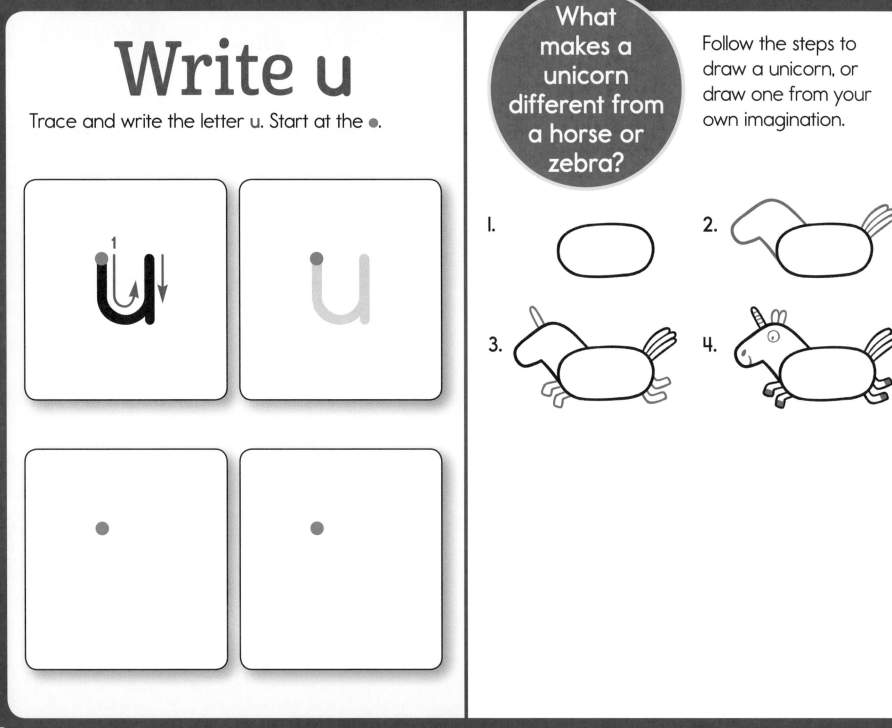

What makes a unicorn different from a horse or zebra?

Follow the steps to draw a unicorn, or draw one from your own imagination.

1.

2.

3.

4.

Write v

Trace and write the letter v. Start at the ●.

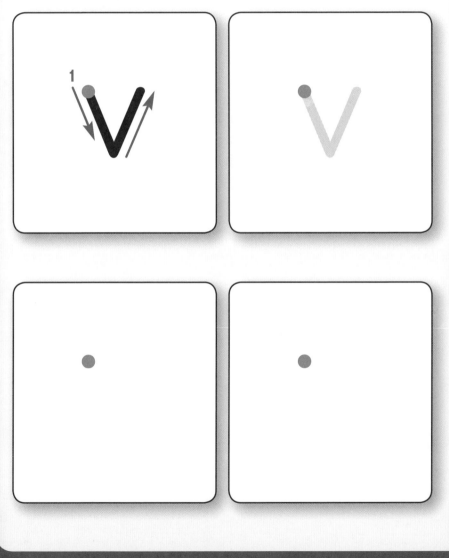

Find and circle the **6** objects in this Hidden Pictures® puzzle.

Which vegetables are green?

cloud   wishbone   umbrella   tennis ball   cork   cane

Write w

Trace and write the letter w. Start at the ●.

Draw a line to help each walrus reach its friend.

Can you think of another animal that starts with w?

Write x

Trace and write the letter x. Start at the ●.

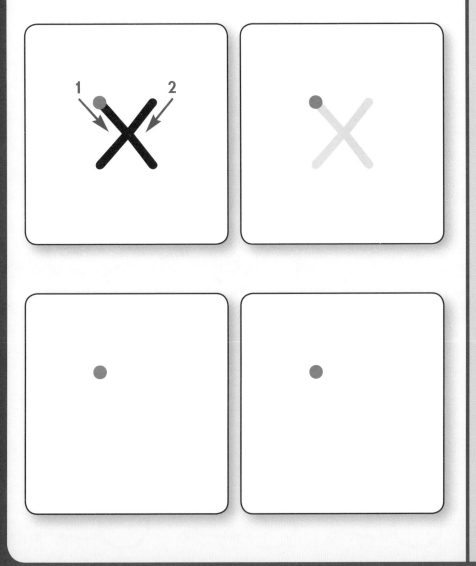

Draw a line from each fox to the one that looks the same.

Can you think of 2 words that rhyme with fox?

Write y

Trace and write the letter y.
Start at the •.

Find and circle the **5** yo-yos in this picture. Color the yo-yos below as you find them.

Write z

Trace and write the letter z. Start at the •.

Draw a path to help Zack the zebra find his father.

What other animals are black and white?

START

FINISH

Alphabet Find

Find and trace all the uppercase
and lowercase letters of
the alphabet.

M A
E Y
T Y
L
E E
K
L
I i O p
o
K
H a R r j
S H R
c
v j f
U
D m e B x P
W

What silly things do you see?

Write 1

Trace and write the number 1. Start at the ●.

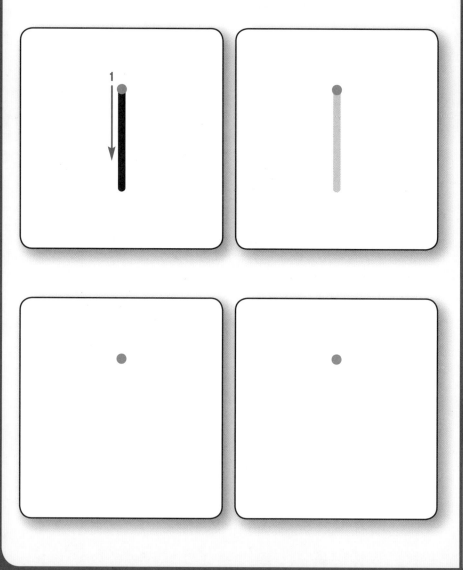

Draw a ◯ around 1 🐞. Draw a ___ under 1 🐞.

Draw a ▢ around 1 🪲. Draw a △ around 1 🐌.

Draw an ✕ on 1 🐛.

Write 2

Trace and write the number 2. Start at the •.

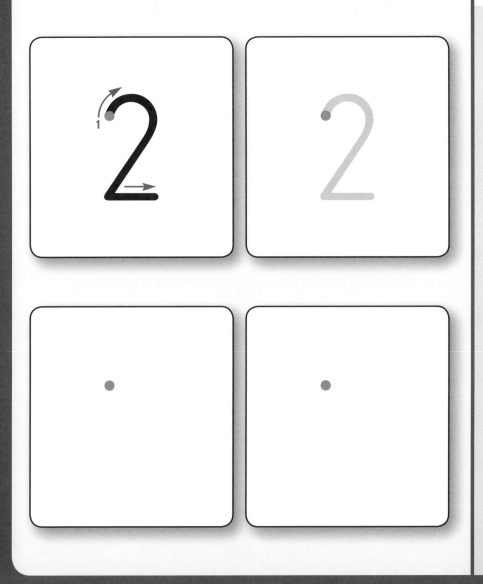

Find and circle **2** eggs in the top picture. What other groups of **2** can you find?

Circle the differences you see between these pictures.

Write 3

Trace and write the number 3. Start at the ●.

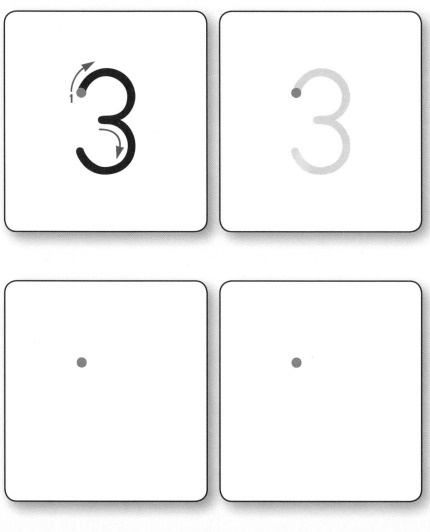

Count the number of fish in each fish tank. Write the number. Draw a line from each tank to the tank with the same number of fish.

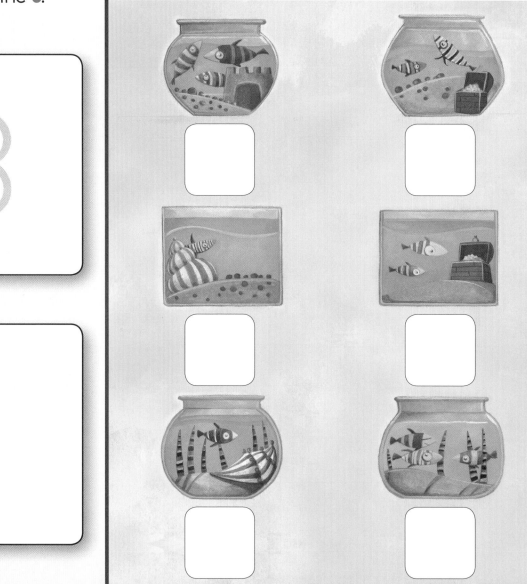

Write 4

Trace and write the number 4. Start at the ●.

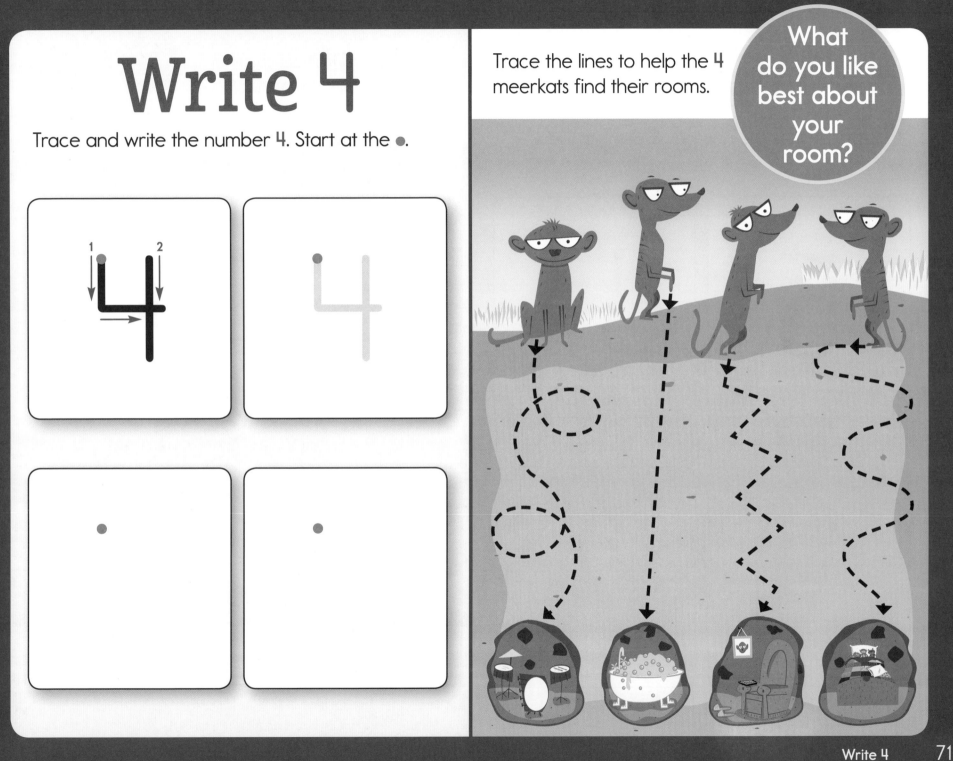

Trace the lines to help the 4 meerkats find their rooms.

What do you like best about your room?

Write 5

Trace and write the number 5. Start at the ●.

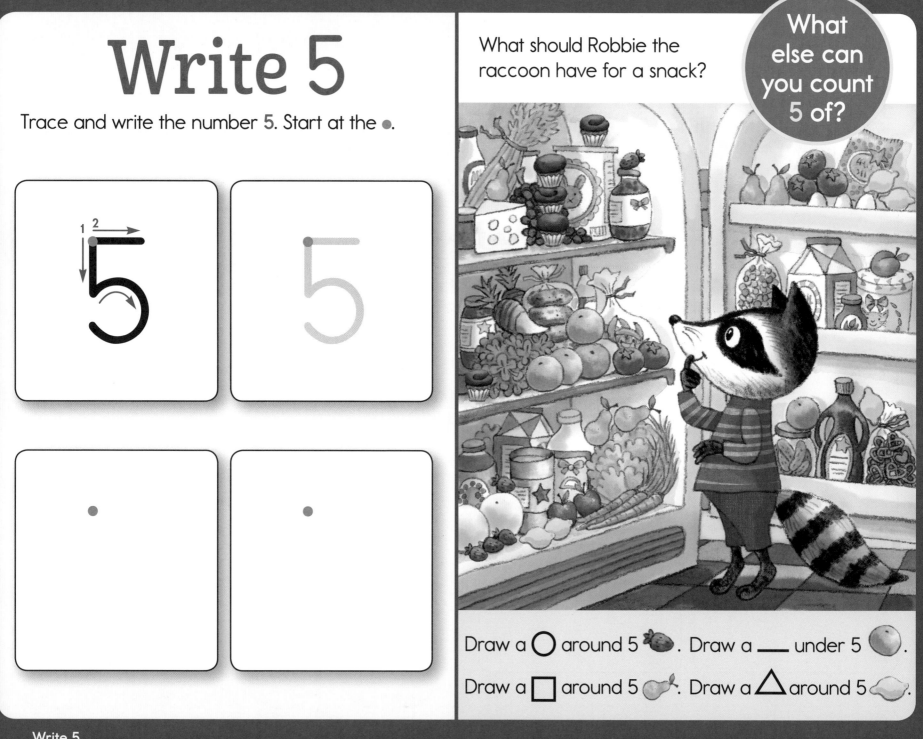

What should Robbie the raccoon have for a snack?

What else can you count 5 of?

Draw a ◯ around 5 🦐. Draw a ___ under 5 🍊.
Draw a ☐ around 5 🍐. Draw a △ around 5 🍋.

Write 6

Trace and write the number 6. Start at the ●.

Find and trace 6 6's in the picture.

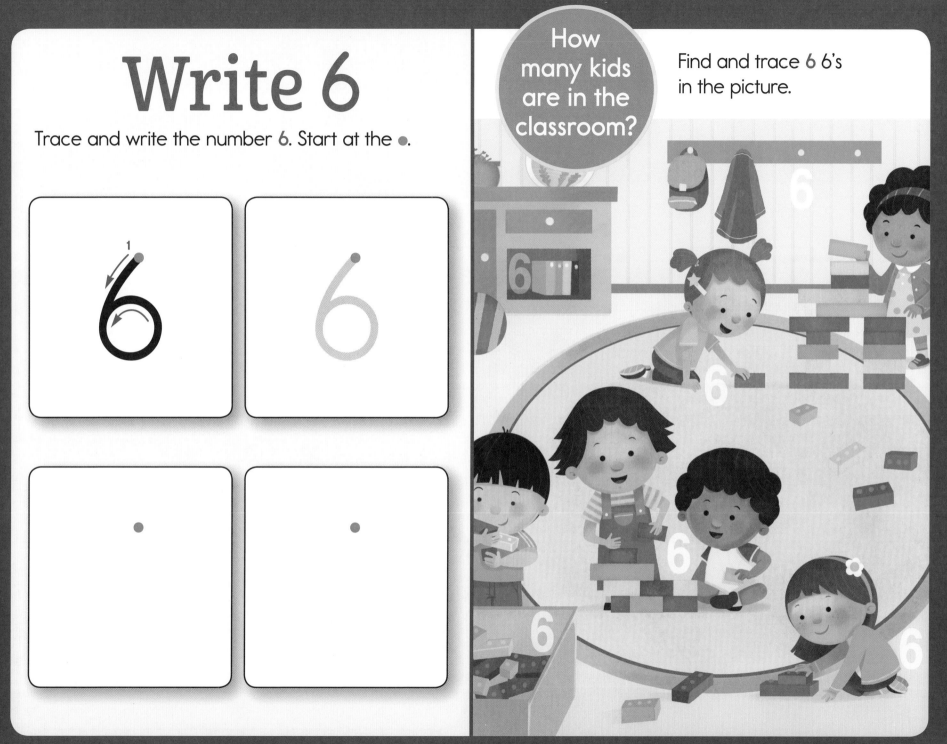

Write 7

Trace and write the number 7. Start at the ●.

Can you also find a T for tiger? Write other letters you see.

Find and trace 7 7's in the picture.

Write 8

Trace and write the number 8. Start at the ●.

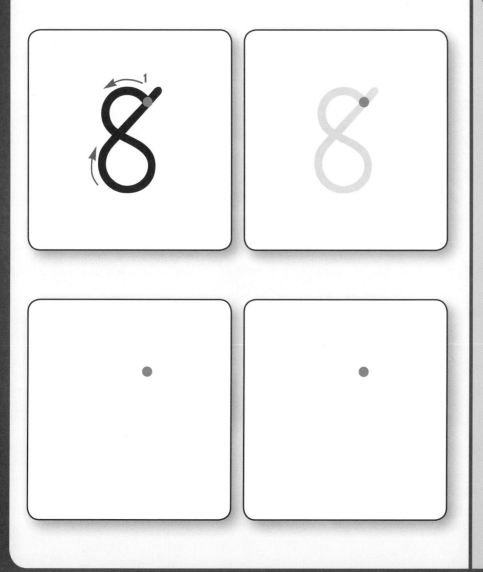

Write 9

Trace and write the number 9. Start at the ●.

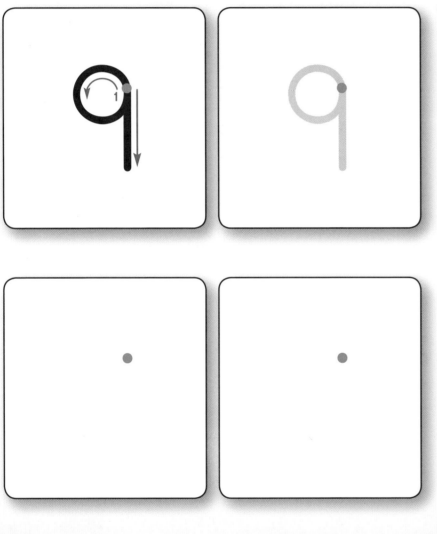

Find and circle 9 balloons in the picture. Then trace and color each balloon below.

Write 10

Trace and write the number 10. Start at the ●.

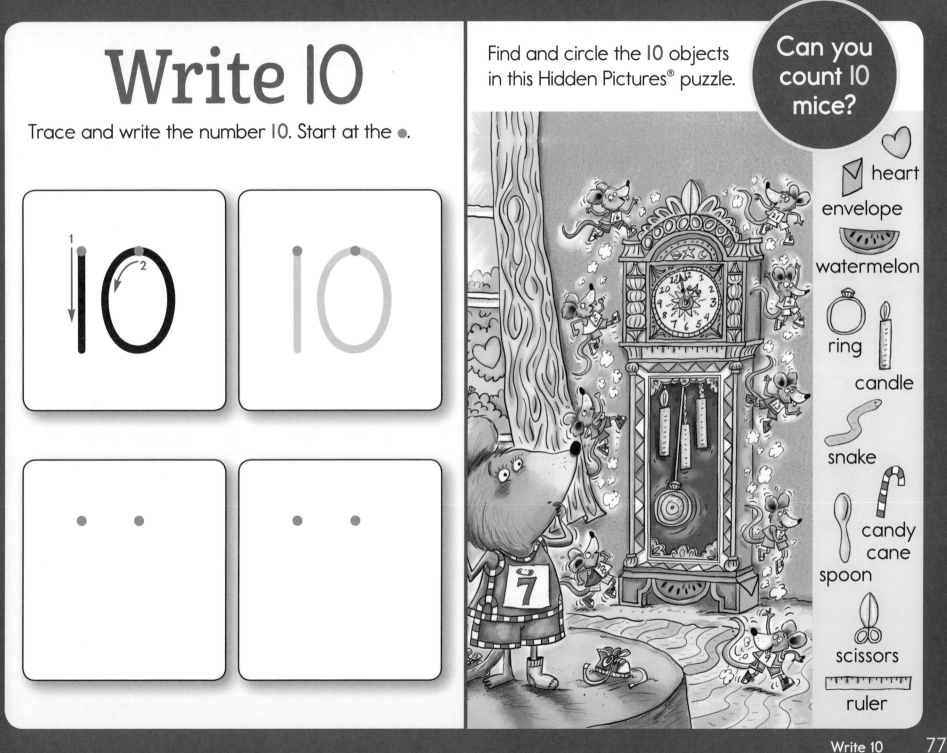

Find and circle the 10 objects in this Hidden Pictures® puzzle.

Can you count 10 mice?

heart

envelope

watermelon

ring

candle

snake

candy cane

spoon

scissors

ruler

Answers

Page 5 – Left or Right?

Page 15 – Write B

Page 16 – Write C

Page 18 – Write E

Page 20 – Write G

Page 21 – Write H

Page 25 – Write L

Page 27 – Write N

Page 28 – Write O

Page 30 – Write Q

There are 11 Q's.

Page 31 – Write R

Page 33 – Write T

Page 35 – Write V

Page 37 – Write X

Page 40 – Write a

Page 41 – Write b

Page 44 – Write e

Page 45 – Write f

Page 46 – Write g

Page 48 – Write i

Page 49 – Write j

Page 55 – Write p

Page 56 – Write q

Page 58 – Write s

Answers

Page 59 – Write t

Page 61 – Write v

Page 63 – Write x

Page 64 – Write y

Page 65 – Write z

Page 69 – Write 2

Page 70 – Write 3

Page 72 – Write 5

Page 73 – Write 6

Page 74 – Write 7

Page 75 – Write 8

Page 77 – Write 10